Balancing the Single Mom Budget

April McCaffery

ISBN:1523694165
ISBN-13:9781523694167

CONTENTS

Introduction vi

Step One: Stop Incurring New Debt 1

Step Two: Budget Your Money on Hand 3

Step Three: Values Summit 6

Step Four: Track Your Spending 8

Step Five: Refine Your Budget 12

If You're Going to School 27

Increasing Income 31

Step Six: Live on Last Month's Income 33

From Surviving to Thriving 35

INTRODUCTION

My official life as a single mom started in June 2003. We were living in Rochester, NY, and I used my tax refund that year to buy plane tickets for me, my two daughters (just a few months shy of their 3rd and 6th birthdays) and my cat to move back home to L.A. I had just turned 30, I had no car, no job, terrible credit and was moving back in with my parents after leaving my husband. I had been married to a drug addict and the last straw was when he took the cash I'd hidden for groceries to buy more drugs. Not the first time, but it would be the last. The only things we took with us were clothes and my daughters' stuffed animals.

I wish I could say that I never incurred debt again. But I can't.

I worked a temp job that hired me on permanently in October 2003, and moved into a 1-bedroom apartment that December. Our department usually participated in a Secret Santa for deserving families; Christmas 2003, we were that family.

A good thing too, because we needed everything. Thanks to my employer's credit union, I plunked down my shiny new credit card to buy beds for the girls and a refrigerator. Everything else was a hand-me-down or a Secret Santa Christmas gift. The girls got the bedroom and I slept on a futon in the living room.

So why should you read this book to improve your own financial situation? Because I have been there.

I scoured the internet for resources to help me. Because I had a decent-paying job, I didn't qualify for government assistance for very long. But living in L.A., "decent" is a relative term. While the court ordered child support, actually receiving it from a drug addict who rarely has the same home address for long certainly doesn't hold a job long enough for any agency to collect. He would give me some, sometimes, but never anything that I could (or should) count on.

We pulled ourselves up by the proverbial boot-straps. Eventually, I went back to school (my parents watched the girls; one of the advantages of moving back to L.A.) and I was lucky enough to work for someone who recognized and rewarded efforts and got promoted. But because I am someone that started my single mom journey without a college degree, living in an expensive city, with no child support, I know you can, too.

At the beginning, I thought this single mom thing would be temporary. But the longer I was a single mom, the less I could imagine bringing someone else into the picture. Whether you're a single parent for a year or 10 or 20, a single parent can only plan with what there is. If/when it changes, you'll re-examine, but for now, financially plan for the life you have today.

I hope you can learn from my mistakes and my victories. I am not a certified financial planner, but I have managed to get myself out of credit card debt, living on last month's income, and my experience will be far more valuable than yet another "tip" on skipping morning lattes. I want to throw coffee at someone when I hear that, too!

STEP ONE: STOP INCURRING NEW DEBT.

I know it's harder to do than say. Becoming credit card debt-free took longer than I wanted, thanks to a $1400 car repair. At the same time, I know that particular car repair was the one that finally convinced me it had to stop once and for all.

I had paid down my high-interest credit card debt to zero, and I was determined never to use it again. Except when the call came about how much that car repair would be, I really had no choice but to use it. I didn't have an emergency fund. My lower-interest credit card did not have enough available to cover the car repair cost. My only other option would have been to take out a 401(k) loan, but I didn't even think of that at the time. When the call comes and you know you have to pick up your kids from school in a few hours, your brain has enough going on. You can't think of anything else to do but to pull out the credit card.

But it tortured me that I was back in the same place again, mere months after shouting to the world, I paid off that credit card!!

The problem was I shouldn't have paid that card off in the first place. I should have kept at least $1,000 aside for the unexpected emergency. I probably could have come up with the remaining $400 by scraping by for a few weeks if I had $1,000 sitting in my savings account. But I didn't.

The real key to not incurring any new debt is to set aside emergency money. Dave Ramsey recommends $1,000. I think that's a good starting point.

You may not have $1,000 the day you read this, and that's okay, too. Still make it your goal to not incur any new debt; especially credit card debt, but really, any debt.

For now, just make your minimum payments on the cards and if you were throwing any extra money to your debt, set it aside instead to your Emergency Fund until you hit that $1,000.

If you were planning on spending $200 at the grocery store and only spent $180, set that $20 aside for your $1,000. Because once you have that, it will become much easier to never incur new debt again.

You don't have to cut up or freeze your credit card (although you may want to), but at least take it out of your wallet and leave it in a safe, but not easily accessible place. Make it harder on yourself to incur new debt than it is to stay out of it.

Activities

Look at your last 6 months – 1 year credit card statements. No, don't go digging through your filing cabinet, look them up online! Look for patterns. Do you always spend more than you expected at Target? Maybe stay away from there for a while. My problem areas were Christmas, the girls' birthdays, car maintenance, and the kids' summer program. Make note of your own problem areas.

Hide your credit card from yourself! Put it in a shoebox in the top of your closet. Freeze it. Stick it between used checkbooks. Just get it out of your wallet and out of easy reach.

Do not incur new debt. Not today, not tomorrow, not next month or next year. No. New. Debt. Period.

STEP TWO: BUDGET YOUR MONEY ON HAND TO GET YOU THROUGH UNTIL YOUR NEXT PAYCHECK

You Need a Budget (youneedabudget.com – also known as YNAB) teaches budgeting this way. You ask yourself: what does this money need to do before I get paid again?

When I was living paycheck-to-paycheck, I would create transactions in my register to account for the pro-rated amount needed from that paycheck for most of my monthly bills.

Example: I am paid weekly. Each paycheck, I would set aside ¼ of my monthly rent.

If you're paid twice monthly, you'll do so for half the amount due. Use this method for your rent/mortgage, your utilities (including internet, cell phones, etc.), car payments, student loan payments and even your credit card payments. If you can, go ahead and pay that pro-rated amount towards your credit card minimum (it can help even slightly with your interest). With fluctuating monthly payments like gas and electricity, just use last month's bill to guestimate. Also, most utilities now offer a level payment plan so that your electricity bill doesn't skyrocket in the summertime so look into getting on the level payment plan instead. It definitely helps manage paycheck-to-paycheck living!

Then, budget how much you'll need for groceries and gas/transportation until your next payday.

Still have unbudgeted money? Great, throw it at your emergency fund until you hit $1,000!

If you already have $1,000, start pro-rating the annual & semi-annual bills: car registration, insurance, Christmas gifts, birthday gifts, summer child care, kids' activities registration, gym membership, Costco membership, Amazon Prime membership. Divide each amount due by the number of months until the bill will come due. You now have a "monthly" bill for each of them.

Still have unbudgeted money? Great, now set aside some for stuff you'll forget: car repairs, co-payments, all known as Rainy Day Funds. It doesn't have to be a lot. I fund my category known as "Mayhem" at $25/month. It gives you a little wiggle room.

Still have unbudgeted money? Now, you can buy the pizza! Or take the kids to the movies. Or buy yourself a latte ☐ .

Note: If you haven't yet hit $1,000 in your Emergency Fund, don't worry about those last three paragraphs just yet. Your goal is simply to build until you reach there, and not incur any new debt. Period. Once you hit $1,000, then you can start budgeting for the non-monthly expenses.

Activities

Budget all the money you have.

<u>Worksheet</u>
Checking account balance: _____
Savings account balance: _____
Total available to budget: _____
Rent/Mortgage (1/_ of $[total due]: _____
Gas/Water/Refuse (1/_ of $_____: _____
Electric Co (1/_ of $___: _____
Internet (1/_ of $__): _____
Cable TV/Netflix/Hulu (1/_ of $__): _____
Cell Phones (1/_ of $__): _____
Home Phone (1/_ of $_): _____
Car Payment (1/_ of $___): _____
Credit Card 1 Minimum Payment (1/_ of $__): _____
Credit Card 2 Minimum Payment (1/_ of $__): _____
Student Loan Minimum Payment (1/_ of $__): _____
Other Monthly Bill _____ (1/_ of $__): _____
Other Monthly Bill _____ (1/_ of $__): _____
Other Monthly Bill _____ (1/_ of $__): _____
Transportation ('til next payday): _____
Groceries ('til next payday): _____
Emergency Fund: _____
*Non-monthly bills (1/__ of $_____): _____
*Rainy Day funds: _____
*Entertainment/Eating Out/Fun Money: _____
Total available income to budget minus total budgeted should equal $0.
This is known as zero-based budgeting. You budget every dollar.

*If you do not have any money left to budget to the starred categories, you have already budgeted every dollar and right now, there are simply no dollars to budget to these areas. Later, we will look at how to cut these areas, but this is where you are right now. Today. Ensuring that your basic needs are met and monthly bills are paid and that you are putting away towards your Emergency Fund will help ensure that you never incur new debt again.

STEP THREE: VALUES SUMMIT

Okay, so you might be a little overwhelmed right now, seeing just how far your income has to stretch. And you might have noticed that there is a lot that's not covered above: clothing, vacations, allowances, haircuts, to name a few. We'll get there.

Right now, we're going to take a step back. We're not going to worry so much about the numbers, but where that money is actually going.

@longstockinggirl hosted a Values Summit on the YNAB Forum. Here's what you do.

You're going to take all of your spending categories and figure out what you value. What is most important to you and your family? What makes it worth getting up in the morning? We all know that money doesn't buy happiness, but what does your money buy that brings joy or value to your life?

This is where personal finance gets personal. For me and the girls, it's going to see musicals. Yes, they are totally overpriced, but we value these experiences. Usually, I look for deals on Goldstar.com, but every so often, there's a musical that comes to town where I don't want to wait to see if half-price tickets become available. Frankly, you could not pay me to go to a football game! This is what our family personally values.

Activity

Take index cards, post-it notes or tear notebook paper into quarters, and write down all of the categories where your money goes. Use your last few bank and credit card statements for reference – again, should be available online. Include rent/mortgage, utilities, eating out, your kids' summer camp, vacations/travel, memberships and dues, haircuts, clothing, groceries, holiday decorations, gifts, etc., everything you can think of.

Pick your top 10: what do you value most? Use the cards/paper to arrange them in order, and once you're satisfied with your top 10, list them (either analog or in a Word doc).

Some people spend lots of time on this, but I find going with your gut instinct works best.

Then, pick your top 11-20, then 21-30 and so on.

Save this list and we'll come back to it later. If you forget something, just go back to your list when you think of it and figure out if it belongs in the top 10 or lower.

STEP FOUR: TRACK YOUR SPENDING TO STAY ON BUDGET

There are a few different methods for tracking your spending. You want to pick the method that's easiest for you and one you can see yourself actually doing. Yes, this is another area where personal finance is personal. The apps may appeal to a techie, but scare the heck out of someone who still has a flip phone. Below are just a few possible tracking methods. Google is your friend for finding others, or may inspire you to create your own tracking system (which will make it more motivating to actually track).

3x5 spiral notebook: Take each of your flexible spending categories (i.e., not your fixed monthly bills) and name them on the top of each page. Write down the amount you have budgeted until your next paycheck. Do this for groceries, gas, spending money, and even your non-monthly bills if you've gotten that far.

When you spend from a category, subtract the amount spent and write down your new total.

Example:

Groceries

$100

-80 (name of store: date)

Total: 20

The actual tracking may be hard at the beginning. While I highly recommend doing it as you spend, I know that's easier said than done. The system you use can make this easier or harder. If one system isn't working for you, try another. But at least give yourself a week with a system before you switch.

One time, I was determined to enter the amount spent on gas as soon as I sat back down in the car. But it was morning rush hour, and there were cars waiting to fuel up, so I drove off instead and entered it when I got to work.

The 3x5 notebook is easy to carry in my purse so I would enter it at work, and check it again that night before bed, and again in the morning after checking my balances online. Yes, I got a little obsessive about it! But frankly, I enjoy knowing exactly how much I have.

The next time you get paid, add the new budgeted amount to the remaining total (if any). If you don't go to the grocery store again until your next paycheck, the next few lines may read like so:

+80 (4/15 paycheck)

Total: 100

Note that I only budgeted 80 this time instead of 100 since I still had 20 left. That's one of the decisions you'll need to make when budgeting new income. You may decide to only budget $60 this time. Or, you may want to stock up on something so you budget a total of $120 until your next paycheck.

Since these are the flexible spending categories, allow yourself this opportunity to be flexible in your spending.

So what happens if you actually spent $120 when you only budgeted $100? That $20 has to come from somewhere. So you look at your other flexible spending categories and figure out where you can move $20. Maybe you just filled up your gas tank and won't need more until your next payday and there's still $30 in there. So on the gas category page, you would enter as follows:

Total: $30

-$20 (to groceries)

Total: $10

On the Groceries page, you would enter

+$20 (from Gas)

Total: $120

-$120 (Ralphs)

Total: $0

You didn't incur new debt, so your budget is still working for you. A budget is a tool for your personal finances. It is not, in fact, set in stone, but the key is to continue using it, even when things don't go as initially planned.

For more years than I'd care to admit, I thought I was budgeting, and even tracking, but I wasn't changing the budget as I went. If I went over, then I'd consider the budget "blown" and what difference is this additional debt going to really make? I'm already in debt, and I'm never going to get out because this always happens.

I also get that, chances are, you are not overspending on items for yourself. Your kid calls and tells you she needs 3-fold poster board for a school project. That's due tomorrow. Or you have to pay out of pocket for a co-pay because you've already maxed out your flexible spending account for the year and your child gets an ear infection on December 29. These are the sort of things that would blow my budget every month. And every month, I thought, next month will be different.

Well, I'm sorry but feel it's my duty to tell you, there is no such thing as a normal month. It's always something. From the car registration to kids' school supplies, Christmas, your cousin's wedding or baby shower, Spring Break, every month there will be something that was different from the last. So the budget has to allow for that.

For now, use the flexibility of your flexible spending categories to get you through. Maybe it's buying stew beef instead of a pork loin for dinner. Maybe you can start carpooling once a week to cut down on your gas.

My first "sacrifice" was making my lunch to take to work. I started with just three times a week. I was taking my lunch more often than not. Then it was on days I didn't have lunch plans with friends. Well, a few of those days, my lunch plans would get rescheduled or canceled, so I started bringing it even if I did have lunch plans. If I went out to lunch, the lunch I brought could stay in the fridge overnight at work and it was one less thing I had to think about the next morning. Assuming an average of $5 per lunch and bringing it 4 days a week (minus two weeks' vacation), I'm saving $1,000 a year simply by bringing my lunch. That's an Emergency Fund!

Sacrifice was in cutesy quotes because most days, I was annoyed with the whole concept of trying to decide where to eat, what to eat, waiting in line, and yes, even spending too much money on a meal I didn't love, just kept the hunger pangs away. In the beginning, it's hard to change habits, but the more you pay attention to where your money is going, the more your feelings about it may change.

Check in with your values list as you are tracking. You may find you're spending in areas that really don't matter to you, as I did with lunches.

Single parents are always looking to save time, too, so I thought it was an even trade, but once I really resented spending that money, I was able to create a system that doesn't take up too much time, and saves me money.

If taking your lunch to work feels like too big a sacrifice, just try bringing your lunch one day a week. If you can work up to three days a week, you are still saving $60 a month. That's my internet bill!

You Need a Budget (or YNAB): I considered this budgeting app my graduation from the notebook to this software. It does the math for you, and follows the zero-based budgeting methodology. You can use the app on your iPhone or Android and the iPad app has even more robust features.

The catch: it's a monthly subscription service for about $5 a month (but I find it totally worth it). You can download a free 34-day trial first before buying. YNAB also offers free training classes.

There is also a robust and helpful community forum. You can follow along other people's journals and ask questions of other forum members.

You can import transactions directly from your bank, but this is completely optional. Even if you import, it is strongly recommended that you continue to manually enter transactions (which YNAB will match when importing). You want to be hands-on about this. Personally, I check my account online every day and reconcile about once a week. Staying engaged and aware of your money helps prevent mathematical errors. Also, by checking in frequently, if there's a fraud charge, you'll know about it sooner, and the sooner you can start fixing it!

Mint: It's free, but in my opinion, you get what you pay for here. Mint does require access to your online account information, but it cannot make changes to your bank or credit card accounts. Mint is good at giving you snapshots of your money. The budgeting tool, however, is not as facile and flexible as you get from YNAB or even your spiral notebook. I've found this to be true of every other tracking program I've tried besides YNAB.

Cash Envelope System: Your parents or grandparents may have budgeted this way. Each category goes in its envelope. You physically move money from envelopes if you want to make changes. You can write down the tracking info on the envelope or in a piece of paper inside. This method works for a lot of people, but I have never personally tried it because I don't want to be carrying all that $$ around, or not have the right envelope(s) with me when I need them.

Excel spreadsheet: Those years that I thought I was budgeting and tracking, I was using an Excel spreadsheet. YNAB started as an Excel spreadsheet, and there are plenty of forms and templates available online. Once you have your formulae in place, changes can be made easily and accurately in Excel. It's essentially free since you've already paid for the program. The catch is accessibility. Programs like Google Docs and cloud services make this easier, but it's just not how my brain works.

I use an Excel spreadsheet for my grocery budget, and I end up emailing the latest and greatest to myself on Gmail so that I have it at home or work. For my entire budget, however, I much prefer YNAB.

Obviously, my biases are clear here, but again, this is just a small sample of what's available for tracking your spending. There are plenty of options available at plenty of price points. The key to this personal finance tool is finding the one that you will actually use. And then, of course, using it.

STEP FIVE: REFINE YOUR BUDGET

The previous steps have given you valuable information to hone, refine, and finesse your budget so that you can finally start feeling like you're getting ahead!

Prior to her political life, Elizabeth Warren (a former Harvard professor) and her daughter Amelia Warren Tyagi wrote two books on personal finance that changed the conversation.

I first read The Two-Income Trap because I was a single parent. I knew that most families with two working parents were still struggling, and if I could better understand why they were struggling, maybe I could learn something about how to improve my own situation.

They found that the top 3 reasons for bankruptcy were job loss, divorce, and health issues. And because families were counting on both incomes, any one of those things devastated their finances.

In All Your Worth, Warren and Tyagi came up with a solution that can be particularly useful to single parents: the 50/30/20 budget.

Only 50% of your income should be going towards your must-haves: your rent/mortgage, your utilities, groceries, insurance and contractual monthly obligations – except your credit card bills.

(Before you throw this book across the room, let me explain that I do not expect this to be your actual budget within the next month or so: it is a goal.)

30% can be spent on Wants: Netflix, your kids' activities, eating out, magazine subscriptions, whatever you and your family want.

20% of your income should go towards Savings, which includes your debt payments. (Warren states that student loan payments should be included in your 50%, but again, I'm being realistic about this. A mortgage, of course, would have to go to the 50% Must-Haves.) Once your debt is paid off, then the full 20% of your income should be saved for emergencies and retirement.

These are great goals, for single parent families especially! And if I'd known about this method years ago, there are some choices I may have changed. But I didn't, so here I am, with 67% of my income going towards Must-Haves. I have to be honest about this. But I am implementing new goals so that eventually, I can get closer to this ratio. You can still progress greatly if you're reaching towards this method.

I am, however, starting my daughters off on the right foot. They know the 50/30/20 formula and agree that it's the best way to manage their finances when the time comes. Both my girls are incredibly wary of debt. My youngest is already trying to figure out how to pay for college without student loans!

While we are working to ensure our own financial future, it's important to recognize that the better we get at this, the better we can teach our own children financial habits that they can implement for more secure financial lives for the rest of their lives.

So how do you get closer to this 50/30/20 goal? By tackling the bigger expenses and the monthly expenses, and putting any savings we find into our Emergency Savings, our Rainy Day funds, and our retirement savings.

We had been living the same place that I never loved for about 7 years before they raised our rent. I decided to shop around, and ended up finding a place I do love for the same rent prior to the increase. Yes, there were moving costs, but I kept my monthly payment at the same rate instead of increasing it (and had enough put away to cover the moving costs without incurring new debt).

If you are renting, anytime they raise the rent, go ahead and look. Hopefully, by the time that happens, you will have enough socked away so that you can manage the moving expenses and then save money by moving. Yeah, it's a hassle, but it's less depressing than seeing more than your annual raise go to your landlord! We can't get ahead if we keep increasing our costs.

CoAbode is a service that connects single parent families to share residence. There can be some great benefits to this beyond the money saved. Your kids can grow up with other kids. You can have another parent there to talk to and share your parenting challenges and triumphs. You might be able to help each other out with carpooling and babysitting. You can take turns cooking dinner so that neither of you are cooking every night. Or one of you can cook and the other one can clean!

Of course, there are disadvantages, too, and those kept me from ever doing so myself, but it's certainly something to consider.

If you are a home-owner, shop around for cheaper home insurance whenever you get notice of your renewal.

And if you're a car-owner, do the same with your auto insurance.

If you are a renter that hasn't looked into renter insurance, please do so!

I was finally convinced after hearing the episode of the MoneyBuzz podcast where one of them had her laptop stolen right under her fingertips (literally) and she learned if she had renter's insurance, they would have covered her replacement! Instead, she's still making monthly payments on a laptop she no longer owns. Minutes after listening to that, I called my auto insurance company and got renter's insurance that cost less than my Netflix subscription! For renter's insurance, the discount makes it worth it to bundle, so do both car and renter's with the same company…and during your renewal period, get at least three quotes before you re-up for the next 6 months or year.

Cell phones: Slowly but surely, I am weaning each of us off Verizon and getting us onto Republic Wireless.

I chose Republic Wireless for the unlimited texting (because I have teenagers), but Ting might be an option for you.

First and foremost, it's not a long-term plan so if I happen to find something even cheaper elsewhere, I don't have to wait out a contract.

I am paying just under $12 (when you include the taxes) for my unlimited talk/text plan with wi-fi. The catch? You have to use their phones. So I saved up, but had the funds available when my contract expired to move to Republic Wireless and immediately started saving money.

It's not a perfect service. There have been some dropped calls or crazy noises if the service is switching from cell to wi-fi, but for my usage, I'm totally fine with that.

Of course, keep in mind even if your kids are little now, they will become teenagers, too! You will either want a plan that includes their usage or allows you to block them from using it in a way that makes you pay dearly for it!

One of my bosses once got a $700 cell phone bill when one of his daughters was a texting teenager. We all learned from that experience.

Now, there are apps that kids today use to text, but I'm too exhausted to figure those out. So this was our solution, and it works for us.

Cable/Satellite TV. It took us years, but finally (!), we cut the cable cord (or, more factually, satellite). It helps that there are more services available now. For us, Netflix, Hulu and Amazon Prime put together still cost us $55 less than what was our monthly satellite TV bill. We were already paying for Netflix and Amazon Prime prior to cutting cable, so my monthly expenses dropped by $76 when I made the cut.

Since then, SlingTV has come out for $20 a month and who knows what will be available by the time you read this! I decided not to get SlingTV because for us, it would mean adding to my monthly bills, so be careful about adding too many a la carte services.

Groceries: I have tried many methods, and what finally worked for us was budgeting $5/day/person. Most months, it's $465. I had been trying for $100 a week, but would always "fail." Turned out, it's because I wasn't budgeting enough. You want to be realistic - and not starve.

I have found menu planning to be the best and easiest way to stay on or under budget. I pick items for the week using Pepperplate.com (it's free), and I bought the ValueTracker app (.99/ios only) to track prices. After I've added the items from the menu, I also add the other stuff we need that week: beverages, snack foods, hair conditioner, etc. I check the estimated total on the app, and if I'm too close to my budget, I may switch one of the menu dinners for something more reasonable, or delete a snack food or two if I'm not that far off. Prior to getting the app, I maintained an Excel spreadsheet (one tab per store) and updated it after every shopping trip, using the receipt. It's actually less time-consuming than it sounds.

It may help to designate themes to each night of the week. Monday: Pasta, Tuesday: Chicken, Wed.: Breakfast for Dinner, etc. Whatever you can do to make the process of menu planning easier for you will in turn make menu planning a less daunting task.

(Incidentally, I use a similar decision-making process for deciding what I'm going to wear. I wear my pants in the order that they're hung, and then pick the next top that will match. I'm all about simplifying my decisions because I need to save my brain cells for work and parenting!)

I forget about coupons. I had about a dozen coupons for a product I buy almost every week, and only used two of them prior to expiration. If you can keep on top of them, go for it! Having said that, do not buy two or three of something just to use a coupon if it will put you overbudget. Do not try a new brand just to use a coupon as store brands are often cheaper all the time. You don't want to get hooked on something that will cost you more money next week. I do much better with store coupons that are emailed to me and then I load them onto my store's card through the store's website. At the actual store, I don't have to do anything other than swipe my card in order to get those discounts! And because these deals are personalized, they are 90% more likely to be for items that I buy anyway. The store is rewarding me for going to that store instead of their competitor.

I also pick up non-menu items at the grocery store (when my daughter needs more index cards, conditioner, hand soap, etc.) and even with those things, I can stay in budget using the $5/day/person method.

Another big help has been the Budget Bytes website and book. For the most part, I don't like cooking, but I enjoy cooking her recipes and I'm usually happy with the results!

I also use the slow cooker at least once a week. My oldest daughter loves beef stew and that can be made fairly cheaply in the slow cooker. I would love to make corned beef more often, but it's not cheap. It's true that going vegetarian cuts grocery costs, but if you have no desire to do that, at least try for one or two meatless recipes a week. Pasta, Mexican and breakfast for dinner are all options that can be meatless and still satisfying.

Obviously, if you can shop without the kids, that helps to cut down on impulse buying!

Your kids will inevitably ask for things that aren't on your list. Involve them in the process and tell them what you will not be buying if you buy their requested item. Let them decide what they want more. (While this won't work with an 18-month-old, it should work for anyone aged 3 and up.)

I also find that sticking to grocery shopping just once a week helps. The only exception is if I forgot but accounted for an item in my budgeting. Always, always *always* shop with a list.

On Costco and other warehouse shopping: enjoy the free samples, but keep your purchases to your list! Also, make note of the price per unit as well as the total. I was buying my K-cups at Costco, and I was good about just getting my K-cups, but hated the hassle. So I was positively delighted when I found a cheaper per unit (and just as good) K-cup option through Amazon's Subscribe & Save!

Amazon's Subscribe & Save is a good alternative to warehouses if you're already a Prime member. There's a 15% discount if you have 5 or more items each month, they show up at your door and you don't have to fight the crowds!

There are also tons of apps available now to comparison shop. Have fun with those if that's your thing, but remember: you're also looking for value in your time! You don't want to drive all over town to save change.

As single parents, time is our most precious resource.

Lunches: I've collected recipes so that I make one recipe on the weekend and eat the same thing for the week: pasta salads, chicken salads, rice with various toppings (this week it's rice with black beans, pineapples & nuts from Budget Bytes). Wraps and sandwiches are also an option. I divide them into containers so that I can just take one and go each day. I also usually bring tortilla chips and a snack bar. While it may sound boring to eat the same thing every day, it's only for one week. Next week will be something different. Also, it keeps me from having to make the decision every single day of what I'm going to eat for lunch. I also save time by only making lunch once a week.

For dinner, freezer cooking has become a big thing too. I confess, I don't do this, but I'm sure Google will give you hours' and even months' worth of freezer cooking ideas. I bring it up because if you find a good sale on meat or poultry, it's a good idea to take advantage and have meals ready in the freezer for a few weeks. (That is, of course, if you have the space! Please do not buy a freezer for the purpose of freezer cooking if it's not something you already do on a regular basis.)

Utilities: I was completely shocked at how much my electric bill went down when I got rid of my "dinosaur" desktop computer and switched to a large-monitor laptop. It saved me about $20 a month! Sometimes, it's worth the cost of investing in later higher-efficiency models than hanging on to an energy-suck. It doesn't have to be the latest and greatest, though. When we moved, I was most excited about buying a washer and dryer (so that I didn't have to deal with coin-operated ones again). I bought used, late model high-efficiency machines and have not incurred an increase to my utility costs as a result.

I also made sure to get on the level paying plan with my gas bill so that I know what my monthly expenditures will be. They get adjusted once or twice a year, and it's usually nominally, but that's much better than not knowing every month!

Cars: Another confession. One of the reasons my Must-Haves is so high is thanks to a car lease. Yep, I have a car lease. It's hard to say whether I would change it or not if I had the chance, because I did have my reasons. The car is electric, and I was spending more on gas each month than I am currently paying for my car lease. I was driving three hours a day because of where my daughters' schools were located and where we lived (and I worked) before we moved. I was constantly worried about our car, which was paid for in full and a Toyota, but I was putting a lot of miles on it and putting a lot of money into it to keep it in good shape. We kept that Toyota, and I'm glad we have two now. I also don't think I would've purchased an electric at that time because of the cost to replace the battery. Electric car technology is improving rapidly, so I liked the idea of having a window of time and experience with electric before buying it outright.

And I do love my new car. I love driving it, I love having electric. I love not worrying all the time about it, and that it's essentially no maintenance!

Cars, bought or leased, new or used, are simply never good investments. They're a tool. They get you and your kids around to all your obligations. The real question is about reliability. It does you no good to buy a 10-year-old car for a song if you're seeing your mechanic every other week, getting this or that fixed. Even if you are knowledgeable about cars and can perform most maintenance yourself, you're still trading away on your time – again, your most precious resource.

Now, I am starting to save money for when my car lease is up. I have not yet decided what I'll do when that happens, but having money available means I will have options. I may buy something used outright, or I may buy a new car with no more than a 3-year term on the loan, and make it a goal to pay it off in less time than that.

If, like me, you're in a lease, there's nothing you can do currently to change it. But keep that in mind, and start putting away even just $20 a month towards what you will do when your lease is up.

If you have a car payment that is killing you financially, do whatever you can to get rid of it. It's almost always a loss when you're selling it, so don't worry about that. The key is to cut your losses, buy something that gets you closer to 50% and move on.

If you do not have a car payment, congratulations! Just be sure you are saving some money towards car maintenance and repairs. My beloved Toyota is still in good condition because I never missed an oil change and deal with problems immediately. When it was my primary car, I worked up to $2000 in a Car Maintenance category so that I didn't have to worry as much. Now, I keep $500 in my Car Maintenance category. The Debt-Free Spending Plan recommends $50-$80 a month for Car Maintenance, depending upon the age and miles on your car.

While in general, most families find a car almost necessary to daily life, you may live in an area where it's not. You may not have a car now! If not, do not make it a goal to get a car. If you are making life work without one, keep it that way. Even though it can sound like freedom, it's really not. Payments, insurance, maintenance, gas, the potential for accidents…

Just the other day, I was at a stoplight watching an Amtrak go by, and I wished I could take that to work. I would love to be able to read or play Words with Friends, or even just look out the window without having to pay attention. I am, of course, not trading in my car, and I appreciate that errands like grocery shopping and getting kids to activities is so much harder when relying on public transportation. I'm just saying, if you are already managing your life without a car, keep doing that until you have enough to either pay a used car outright (plus $500-$2000 available for maintenance and 6-months' worth of insurance) or no more than a 3-year loan. And even though I have a lease myself, I do not recommend you lease a car.

As Warren states in her book, if you can keep your must-haves to 50% of your income, you will be able to sleep much easier at night with the knowledge that you can keep the roof over your head, dinner on the table, and your electricity turned on.

But if you can't? You are so not alone. Most families, even those with two incomes, are not even living within their means, let alone on half their income. Yes, it can be done, but give yourself time to get there.

Debt Repayment/Savings

I would not be out of debt today had I not decided to only pay the minimum due on my outstanding credit card balance. I had at least $8000 due on my credit card when I read The Debt-Free Spending Plan, which changed my life.

I know you're frustrated at how much I'm telling you to save – for your Emergency Fund, Rainy Days, etc. How on earth are you going to do that while you still have debt?

You're only going to pay the minimums for now.

I had thrown every extra dollar I had at debt, and I didn't have anything left over for emergencies. And not even just emergencies, but the "unexpecteds" as I called them. I also didn't have anything for Christmas, birthday parties, new eyeglasses (there was one time my daughter broke her new ones the very day we got them), backpack replacements, and all of the other stuff that comes up when you have kids.

All of those things would go on a credit card and the balance (and minimum payments) would just keep growing.

I know this goes against the advice of many personal finance gurus out there. I'm guessing you're reading this because that advice wasn't working for your family. It didn't work for me, either. I would try so hard to do it the right way. And I would keep finding myself in more debt. That's why The Debt-Free Spending Plan was such a life-changer for me. It gave me the "permission" to try something different. And get different results.

Of course, this only works if you are still practicing Step One every day, every hour of the day. You just cannot incur new debt.

So I did that. I stopped incurring new debt and started just paying the minimum. I used my tax refund to build my Emergency Savings to $1000. With the money I was no longer throwing at trying to pay off my debt faster, I started building my Car Maintenance category. Since I get paid weekly, on those weeks with a 5th payday, that Car Maintenance fund grew bigger, faster.

I *almost* slipped up once when I decided to make a donation to our local Boys & Girls Club. But I could not go to sleep that night until I figured out how to pay it in cash instead. If you do slip up, try and correct it before the credit card bill comes due by subtracting the amount from another category. Yes, even the Emergency Fund, if that's what it takes. But please, do not raid your Emergency Fund every month to take care of overages. You will eventually find yourself back to incurring debt and I know you really don't want to do that.

When my minimum credit card payments started to decrease (because I was no longer adding new debt), I started saving for Girls' Expenses. Then I started a Birthdays category, Christmas, even another Gifts category for Mother's Day, Father's Day, weddings, etc. And my monthly minimum payment on my credit card continued to decrease.

When it got to $150, I stopped checking what the minimum was and just started paying $150 every month. Eventually, getting that debt paid off became my number one priority to me, and I paid it off in full with the tax refund two years after starting this journey.

When it becomes the most important thing to you, absolutely make it your focus. But, in my opinion, it shouldn't be the most important thing until you have your reserves in place. Until the day your kid calls and informs you that you need to buy $50 worth of art supplies and you say "no problem" because your Kids' Category is well-funded for that. Get through at least one Christmas where you paid cash for everything. Get your Car Maintenance category to your goal level.

You have to know that you can stay out of debt once and for all. That will only happen once you've built yourself a nice, comfy cushion for all of the unexpecteds in the life of a single parent.

When you're ready, most of the time, you'll want to pay off the card/loan with the highest interest rate first (while still paying the minimums on your other debts). Once that is paid off, you take the money you were putting towards that debt, and add it to the debt with the next highest interest rate. Lather, rinse, repeat.

Another popular way to pay off debt is known as the "snowball" method. Popularized by Dave Ramsey, this method has you paying the smallest balance first. The reason for this is to help motivate you to keep going with paying off your debt.

Ironically, I ended up being able to use both this snowball and the first method, known as the "avalanche," because my card with the highest interest rate also had the smallest balance. My remaining student loan has the lowest interest rate at 3.25%.

Student loans and mortgages are often taken out of this equation, due to the longer term lengths of the loan. Also, consumer debt in general should come first, as that will be most helpful for your credit score.

You may find yourself wanting to do some combination and that's perfectly okay. If, however, you find yourself just not knowing where to begin, I'd start with the highest interest rate debt first because you will save more money in interest down the road. The decrease in your overall debt should be a motivating factor any way you attack it.

Ideally, this combination of debt repayments and building your cushion(s) will equal 20% of your income. Again, use this as a goal, not an absolute. In the not-so-serious budgeting years and the serious budgeting years alike, I have always set aside about $100 a month to eat out about once a week. Of course, that's usually fast food, but that's okay with us. I enjoy the one opportunity weekly to not make a meal plan, and the girls see it as a treat.

You're raising your kids just once. You don't want to say "no" every single time because that can backfire in the money lessons you're trying to teach your kids. You don't want them to worship or hate money. You want them to understand that it's a tool that gives you options.

My oldest daughter was surprised and delighted when her Christmas gift was a laptop one year. She was sure I couldn't afford it. She only got maybe one other present for her that year, but I knew how much she wanted it, how much she could use it, and I was happy to give it to her. (It wasn't the most expensive laptop on the market, but it was brand new and had plenty of good reviews on Amazon.)

As single parents, we have the added concern of wanting to make up for the absent parent. In my earlier years of the single mom journey, I tried to make up for it by lavishing them with presents and parties. And then I ended up more stressed and upset because of the bills that came with those. I have a blog called It's About Balance. We have to balance our need to compensate with our own personal needs and our family's financial needs. Just as our time is a limited resource, so are our finances.

Go back to your values list, and fund the ones that are most important to the most people in your household.

We love seeing Broadway musicals. The first time I did a Values Summit, Theatre Tickets was in my Top 10. So I made sure it had enough funds so that I could purchase the tickets in the section I wanted (first row, mezzanine) when the national tour of Newsies first became available. I paid $92 a ticket, and was happy to do so. The girls and I looked forward to that for months. When we went, we were so excited and had a wonderful time. It added value to our lives. It was a chance for the three of us to do something special together.

We also love going to The Sound of Music sing-along at the Hollywood Bowl. I'm currently saving for that again this year. These are things that enhance our lives that we talk about for months after. We certainly spend a lot more time appreciating these moments than they remember of what I got them those Christmases and birthdays past when I was lavishing them with quantity instead of quality.

You don't feel guilty about spending money on your family when you're not going into debt to do so. Your children feel like their solo mother is more available to them when she's not freaking out about money. They are also relieved when they call for the 3-fold poster board and you tell them, okay.

The line between wants and needs gets a little blurry when your kid is involved. I found it to be worth it to give them an allowance so that we could refine it.

I pay for their needs out of the Girls' Expenses category. They pay for their wants out of their allowance or their earned income (though I do make my older daughter save 20% of her earned income towards her Emergency Savings). I went ahead and paid for her Grad Night and Prom Ticket and some other senior things because she was just starting her job and I didn't want her to get discouraged, but she paid for her prom dress and spending money for Grad Night.

Having said that, I cut their allowance drastically when I knew I had to do more to get my own financial house in order. I was quite honest with them and explained that I needed to be saving more in my own Emergency Savings in case I lost my job or for retirement. They were 13 & 16 at the time, and they understood that it was also helping them to have the safety net for now, and to ensure that they don't get stuck taking care of me in my old age, too! Just as we have to put on our masks in the event of an airplane emergency first so that we can take care of our kids, we have to have our own emergency money.

Some parents firmly believe in only giving their kids money for chores, others feel some chores should be free and certain ones go over. I tried chore charts and all kinds of things, but none of them really worked for our family. So I decided that they would get this nominal allowance, and it would be our opportunity to talk about money and budgeting and finances. You have to do what's right for you and your family.

Whichever method you choose, do not put yourself in a position of having to give your kids more allowance than you can afford. I gave them more than I should for years until I was getting some financial advice, and the advisor told me, "Why are you doing that? You can't afford that." I knew he was right, but I couldn't heed the advice fully. Instead, we dropped it to $25 a month. It wasn't breaking me, they can't go crazy with it, but I still can use it to say, "I'm not buying that. That's a want. If you want it that bad, save up your allowance for it." Sometimes, they have and sometimes they haven't. Either way is okay because they're making the decision for themselves if they want it enough to pay for it.

Even if they're earning their allowance, make sure they can't earn enough to mess up your budget. Always put a cap on it, let them know the maximum amount they can earn per month, and if they do so, great! If not, put it in your Kids' Category. Trust me, you'll end up using it!

The Kids' Category is difficult to budget properly without the benefit of information. When I had about 6 months' available in YNAB to run a report, I could see that I was spending more than I was budgeting on average (and taking from other categories to make up for it). That was an opportunity to adjust my budget accordingly.

If you are getting child support, the majority should be going in your Kids' Category. You will need it and you will use it. You can use it for dance lessons or sports or just let it grow for college later. The only exceptions are (1) to help pay off debt that you incurred because of the kids, (2) helping to pay for car maintenance (so that you can keep chauffeuring the kids around), or (3) if it's one of your main sources of income. If the latter is the case, you will want to get an 8-month Emergency Fund as soon as humanly possible because it is possible that your ex could lose their job or otherwise stop paying.

If child support is already more sporadic (if at all), just stick it in the Kids' Category. You already know you can't count on it, so don't use it for

Must-Haves. You need to know you can do this on your sole, single income. I know it's frustrating, I know it's unfair, but it's also the reality of your situation.

As you refine your budget, continue to refer to your Values Summit list. This is your money for your family. Every dollar of your money should be going somewhere that you value. You actually do value having a roof over your head (but you may value a cheaper roof), having electricity and yes, even the peace of mind of having your valuables insured properly (not over-insured, just enough). Once those are on auto-pilot, everything else is up to you.

I recommend having a Values Summit every season when you're first starting out, then once a year and every time there's a life change (kids going from middle school to high school; moving; new job, etc.).

Whenever you're able to decrease or cut a monthly bill altogether, first yay! Then, really think about where you want those dollars to go. What would make you sleep better at night? Which category/bucket are you itching to fill? Where you do want to be sure to take your children before they're too old to enjoy it? Where do you want to retire?

Your goals and values may change through the years, so that's why it's important to keep checking in. As your kids grow, your schedules change, where you spend your money will also change. Stay aware of these changes, and let your budget change with you and your family.

Once upon a time, therapy for me and my girls was essential to our budget. Some of it was covered under insurance, but I had to pay some of it out of pocket. I'm glad I did, but eventually, we got to the point where we didn't need it anymore. Once or twice after, something would happen that would bring us back for one or two sessions, but we haven't been back in years now.

Again, I don't enjoy breaking this to you, but I remember thinking that my financial situation would be so much better when I didn't have to pay for day care anymore. Yes, it's great to get that monthly fee back in your pocket, but you will end up spending it in other ways for your kids. Whether it's dance classes, after-school programs, summer camps, new shoes, new uniforms…that will depend on you and your family. And it will no longer be on the regular weekly schedule. The costs will become lumpy, less scheduled.

When their grandmother on their father's side died, another family member was kind enough to pay for the flight for them to attend the services, but that didn't mean it was entirely cost-free to me. Neither of them had appropriate clothes to wear in their current sizes so off to Kohl's we went. We were careful with the prices, but it still cost over $100. The girls were worried for a minute that I would freak, but I was able to say, "it's fine, we have enough."

Not two weeks later, my daughter started her first job! But she needed the right shoes, and she didn't have any money yet since she hadn't started working yet. We went to Payless so it wouldn't be too expensive, and there was more than enough in the Kids' Category to pay for it.

I've read that over their first 18 years, kids cost parents on average 1 million dollars. That number didn't really surprise me. From diapers to day care to high school senior year expenses like Prom and Grad Night, the expenses will be there.

As far as college goes, you have to be sure you're taken care of first before you can take that on. I, quite simply, am not in a position to take that on. My older daughter will work and pay for community college for the first couple of years and then work and take out loans to go to the 4-year program of her choice. I mentioned earlier, my youngest daughter (currently a sophomore in high school) is already looking for scholarships and grants. They know they're on their own when it comes to this. They know I've taken them as far as I can, and they are okay with that.

Of course, I wish I had started this financial journey long ago. Of course, I wish I had a nice fat college fund for both of them. But again, we can't waste too much time beating ourselves up over what ifs. We have to be honest about where we are. And I know I still have a long way to go to get to where all three of us can be assured that I won't be a financial burden on them in the years to come. They know that's my goal, and they support that goal.

They want their future to be free of obligations to me, and so do I. If I gave them every dollar I had in my 401k, that wouldn't be good for any of us. First of all, there's not enough in there to get both of them through college anyway. Second, it would be a terribly unwise financial decision. That money needs to keep growing so that one day, I can retire and I still have to pay off my own student loans. In fact, my youngest daughter wishes I would get more aggressive on that, and I am slowly starting to feel that way, too.

Financial goals can take a really long time. Your emergency savings or 401k (or 403(b) or whatever) won't grow if you keep dipping into it. Find the amount that's comfortable for you and consider it gone. Tell yourself that it's spent because it will be. It will be spent on you when you need it.

I took too long to contribute the max to my 401(k) to the company match. I regret it. When I finally took the plunge, it really didn't hurt all that much, and my 401(k) started growing bigger faster! It's really really worth it.

If you don't have a 401(k), 403(b) or something similar available at work, then after you have at least 3 months of expenses set aside, you can start looking into other options. As stated early on, I am not a certified advisor, so I'm not even going to try! Once you get that savvy, you will enjoy learning about things like Betterment and Vanguard through the myriad of sources available on the worldwide web.

If you want to start really, really small, you might consider Acorns. They round up to the next whole dollar and invest $5 at a time. Example: you spend $34.85 at Amazon. They invest .15 cents.

Speaking of rounding up, this was another trick of mine pre-YNAB. I would never bother with tracking to the nearest penny, but rather the next whole dollar. Again, if I spent $34.85 at Amazon, I would mark it in my check register as $35. If too often you find yourself close to zero in your checking account, then I strongly recommend implementing this strategy at least until you're in a better financial position!

With YNAB, I found it harder to reconcile this way so I stopped; however, I still budget to the nearest whole dollar and then after the bill is paid, I'll add those cents to a savings goal. Alternatively, for my Student Loan payment, I continue to let that account grow and make an extra payment at the end of the year.

You can play these small "tricks" on yourself provided they make your financial life easier. If you're someone who wants to know by the penny, that might not be the case.

Accept Help

Again, in hindsight, I should've started accepting help sooner. From my parents and as the Secret Santa family, I could easily accept help without guilt. But there were other times where I would feel guilty and feel like I wasn't doing enough as a single parent.

If you're a single parent, so long as you're not leaving the kids in the car while you're out partying, you are already doing more than your share. You're the one making the doctor's appointments and signing homework and permission slips, instilling discipline, doing the laundry, making dinner, taking the kids to playdates and birthday parties, buying gifts for those birthday parties, planning your own kids' birthday parties, grocery shopping, helping with homework, listening to the latest friend drama/bad joke/favorite song, imparting advice, enforcing rules, picking up around the house, washing dishes…you are already doing so, so much. Whenever anyone offers to help, say please and thank you.

If someone offers to pay for your lunch, say thank you without protest. I always plan to pay for my own lunch when going out with someone, but if someone offers, I used to go back and forth, and they would still end up paying. Now, I just say thank you and enjoy knowing that money is still available.

There's one attorney who would sometimes just leave an envelope of cash on my desk when I wasn't looking. I used to feel guilty about accepting it. I know she can afford it, I know I didn't ask for it, she just did it because she wanted to. So I finally learned to just say thank you and accept it.

I also had a few friends offer to babysit. This one was also difficult to accept and in the beginning, I would only take them up on it when my parents weren't available. Then I realized that the girls loved spending time with these people, and they loved spending time with my girls. So sometimes, I would ask when it wasn't about school or work, but just to get together with my own friends. I could relax, knowing that my girls were having a good time, as was the babysitter, and so was I. I also learned that my girls were enhanced and enriched by these experiences with other loving adults besides me and my parents.

When we first moved into our own place, at a colleague's urging, I sent an email to everyone I knew personally at work and outside of work, asking them to go through basements for things they no longer needed. I filled up our apartment with the bounty: dishes, a chair, a table, a dollhouse. One friend gave me her futon, which was my bed for a few years. I think they liked giving to someone they knew personally versus donating it to Goodwill. There's a certain set of dishes that was given to me by someone who has become a good friend, and when I pull something from that set out, it makes me think of her and smile. It may be charity, but it's also a win-win. People don't often give away things that they'll miss, and they like knowing that the items are being used.

When you begin to thrive, you may find yourself ready to "pay it forward," and find that giving help is just as (if not more) satisfying as receiving.

IF YOU'RE GOING TO SCHOOL

I finished my BA and got my paralegal certificate while working full-time and a single mom. You may be doing the same.

I do not regret taking out student loans to get through school. It certainly paid off for me in my raises and promotions. Having said that, higher education is getting more and more expensive every semester. Suze Orman says that you should not take out more in loans than you expect to make in your chosen career in the first year. That's probably too optimistic. Still, if you have not started going back to school yet, it's a good idea to run the numbers and see if realistically, the degree will pay for itself in a reasonable period of time.

I considered going to law school after finishing my paralegal certificate. It's something I had always wanted to do, and I thought I would enjoy it. But I ended up deciding not to go for it when I considered the following: even though I have a good chance of being "promoted" to an attorney position, I am simply not comfortable with the level of debt necessary and there are no guarantees. As I get older, I can't help but notice my memory is not as good as it used to be. The last two semesters of getting my paralegal certificate, I was having a tougher time with the rote memorization part of school. Law school has a lot of rote memorization! And finally, I like where I am professionally. I feel like my pay is fair for what I do. As my kids grow older and I have more actual free time on my hands, I want to spend it doing things like writing this and a lot more! I am not in the right head space to be a student right now.

It's perfectly valid to come to the conclusion that school is not right for you right now.

Now, if you are in school and working and you are getting loans, your loans should only be paying for your school-related expenses. They should not be going towards your groceries or rent.

Your disbursement may be different than mine was, but they would send me a check after tuition was paid. I made the mistake of using any remainder on living expenses. I should have been setting that aside. I could have been using it as an Emergency Fund and then eventually paying it back to cut down on the amount owed.

If you have a loan that is accruing interest while you are in school, you should send any unused portion back. If that option isn't available to you, just set it aside for when you can.

Of course, if your student loans are a main source of income right now, you will have to use them on groceries and rent. Still, you should think of yourself as employed, and your "job" is to continue to apply for scholarships and grants while you are in school.

If you are working outside of school, check if your employer has educational reimbursement available. Here's where I was an idiot. Because I wouldn't get reimbursed until after I have passed the class, I would pay on a credit card, and then use the reimbursement to pay the credit card back. What I didn't figure out until the second to last semester of my paralegal school (yeah, I'm slow sometimes), is that I should have been setting aside the reimbursement to pay for the next semester of classes and books!

There are tons of blogs, websites, apps and podcasts that tackle student loans. I've heard multiple experts on financial podcasts. Here are the take-aways:

1. Understand the terms of your loans including repayment options. Ask a bunch of questions, even if you think they sound stupid. Make sure you understand how the loans will be disbursed, when interest begins accruing, and whether or not there are any forgiveness programs. There are public service forgiveness programs, for instance, where your loans are forgiven after working in public service for 10 years (and paying your student loans on the standard repayment plan for those 10 years). These things are good to understand for how you will tackle your student loan payments later. If you know, for instance, you want to work in public service, you might not want to pay extra towards those student loans and focus on other financial goals instead.

2. Run the numbers. Figure out how much you'll need for each semester (including books and supplies), how you will pay for it in the short-term and, if applicable, how you will pay for the student loans in the long term. Know the interest rate and figure out what your monthly payments towards the student loans will be when you have to start paying them back. Also, ask about any discounts that might be available on interest. For instance, I ended up getting 1-1.5% off my interest by enabling the student loan company to directly withdraw the monthly payment from my checking account.

3. Fill out the FAFSA. Even if you don't think you'll qualify for Federal Aid, many scholarship and grants will ask for this info. And you might be surprised to find you do qualify for something. It's free, it's slightly less complicated than a 1040, and there is no downside.

4. Apply for scholarships and grants. Again, even if you don't think you'll qualify, at least look into them. Now, I'm not saying apply for a scholarship for music majors when you're majoring in business, but at least search for scholarships and grants applicable to you and your situation. There are some for single parents, some for your chosen major, your chosen school, possibly your ethnicity or religion. Some of the websites can be overwhelming, so you'll want to start with your school, then your employer, then your community, and finally, apps and websites.

And here are my personal tips for surviving school while being a single parent and working full-time:

1. Do not overload on classes. The whole time, I took it slow and steady. I made sure my schedule was no more than 3 nights a week, and preferably 2 nights a week and one Saturday class. I thought it was going to take me 5 years, but it actually only took 3 years - I was going back so I didn't start from scratch. I think I had enough credits to qualify me as a sophomore when I started back again. Still, even if it had taken me longer, it was worth it to still feel like I had time with my kids and time to actually study! You'll figure each class will require 2-4 hours of work outside the class and you'll want to consider that while making up your schedule. And, if possible, don't take summers off!

2. Make it Homework Time for the Entire Family. All 3 of us would be doing homework after dinner. Sure, mine would get interrupted to help the girls, but I was able to model good study habits by doing my homework alongside them. I would usually still need to finish after they went to bed, but it was a start at least, and it was a way for us to do this together.

3. Enmesh all aspects of your life. I was able to use my life experience as a mother and as an employee within my school work. I interviewed a colleague for one assignment. I wrote about an applicable parenting challenge in another. I used this opportunity to take my skills and knowledge from all areas of my life and roles to enhance and enrich the other roles. Through school, I got involved with a non-profit that had child care available, so one night a week, we would all go where I was both student and tutor (getting college credits), and my daughters got to be a part of the experience. And sometimes, it happened where my girls ended up going to actual college classes with me. It didn't happen often – no more than once a semester, but if my parents were out of town and no babysitter was available, it was just easier to drag them along. They, of course, would have their iPods or other devices and tune out during the class, and get their own homework done or play games. But they never minded having to go, and I kind of liked having them there. (Not every time, of course, but once in a blue moon, it's doable.)

4. If/When Needed, Take a Semester Off. When my oldest started her college prep middle school and I had also just gotten a promotion and more work responsibilities, I decided to take some time off from school. I knew my daughter would need me at night to help get through the homework, and work being crazier, I just wouldn't have the time or energy to go to school on top of it. So I took a break from my Paralegal program – in hindsight, longer than I should have (it does get harder and harder to go back), but eventually, I went back and finished it. And accomplishing that felt great!

INCREASING INCOME

You may find that there is simply not enough. If that's the case, consider finding additional income. I have worked side gigs, and that was also key to getting out of debt faster. I don't include that income when it comes to my regular monthly expenses, but I used it towards paying down my debt and my savings goals. Again, you get to choose where this extra income goes, if you're able to make it. It is hard to find, but there are possibilities.

Babysitting: You can either get paid to watch other kids in addition to your own, or you can do a "swap", where you trade babysitting with another family. Swapping won't get you additional income, but will cut down on your expenses.

Freelance: Use your skills outside of your regular job. Of course, don't jeopardize your day job if there's a non-compete clause in your employment contract, but you may still find ways to translate those skills to a similar area. (Word of mouth/networking is the best way to get these types of gigs.)

Fast food/Retail: If you have free babysitting available in grandparents or friends, you may be able to take on an evening or weekend shift. Be careful not to burn yourself out by working too many hours and feeling like you never get to even see your kids, but one day on the weekends and maybe 1 or 2 weeknights would be doable. Of course, this won't work if you have to pay a babysitter, but if your kids are older, it might.

Sell things online: I hesitate to mention this because there's only so much you already have that you can sell, or you may make things that you can sell on a site like Etsy. If that interests you, then go for it with these two precautions: 1) do not invest too much money in starting something like this because there's no guarantee that it will work (same with starting a blog or other website), and 2) businesses like these require a lot of time on social media that you may not have. Still, if it's something you want to do and hope to one day make into your sole income, then do so slowly and deliberately. Get a business plan in place, read blogs and listen to podcasts that focus on entrepreneurs and plan for setbacks.

There may be times when you receive extra money: a tax refund, a small inheritance (or a large one), or a bonus at work. I like the 1/3 Windfall rule from <u>The Debt-Free Spending Plan</u>: use 1/3 of it towards your debt, 1/3 towards saving, and 1/3 towards something fun. It's a balanced approach that is both responsible, and allows you to actually enjoy it without "blowing" all of it.

STEP SIX: LIVE ON LAST MONTH'S INCOME

Getting off the paycheck-to-paycheck cycle for good was another life-changer for me.

I happen to work at a job where I input my time every week on the company's portal. If I forget to do it one week, I don't get paid (until I enter it, and then get a double paycheck the next week). This is a mistake most people only make once, but still can be costly if it leads to a negative bank balance and the inevitable fees that go with that. Or a missed credit card payment that leads to the highest interest rate allowed for the rest of your life!

Things can also happen quite beyond your control. Your company downsizes or goes under. Your child is sick and you can't work (or get paid). Your payroll department messes up and shorts your check. Your debit card is compromised and you have to fight a fraudulent charge. You're double-charged accidentally. You're moving and have to pay double-rent for a few days or weeks.

Any of those things can wreak havoc on the single parent family that is living paycheck-to-paycheck. Living on last month's income turns all of them from nightmares into annoying inconveniences.

An unexpected bonus allowed me that luxury. And living on last month's income saved me when I forgot to enter my time. It saved me when I had to pay double-rent. And I am no longer living paycheck-to-paycheck.

Over and over in the YNAB Forums, people ask about this rule and where it should go in the priorities. In my opinion, you should get your $1,000 Emergency Fund first, and after that, it's entirely up to you how high a priority. It should, however, be on the list. It will most certainly help you sleep better at night.

That first month was tough because it wasn't entirely the last month's income, but I knew it would be enough for the next month's expenses. I started January 2014. And then all of January's paychecks went to February's budget, and so forth. When I moved and had to pay double-rent for a couple of weeks, I went in the hole on paper (meaning, into that same month's income), but once I got my deposit back, I was back on track.

What you may find is by putting away a percentage of each paycheck, eventually, you will have that amount set aside. This would be the first month of an Emergency Fund. Financial experts go anywhere from 3 months to a full year on how much you should set aside for a job loss or other emergency. Again, it's personal. If you're in a job that does not feel secure, you'll want to save 3 months as soon as possible and then let it build from there. And, really, that's the case for most of us. It's not going to happen overnight. Just so long as you're setting aside some money from each paycheck, and then not taking from it for other things, you will eventually get there.

FROM SURVIVING TO THRIVING

By implementing the steps above, here's where you should be:
• Not incurring new debt, and seeing your credit card minimums decrease;
• Living below your means;
• Increasing your reserves (Rainy Day funds, Emergency funds, Kids' funds);
• Living on last month's income
You are no longer simply surviving as a single parent; you are beginning to thrive!

Now you get to start dreaming about your future and what you want for yourself and your kids. You can start adding back into the budget those things that are beyond the mere necessities of life and start focusing on wants goals rather than needs.

Maybe you can start putting away $50 for the beauty salon or towards a family vacation. You can buy the new coffee maker when yours sputters out without worrying how you will pay for it.

Below is a list of my current financial goals. Some of these will take longer than others, and they're funded with $15 or $20 per month out of my known monthly income, but they are getting funded, and where I throw my additional income from my side gigs and any windfalls.
- New Car
- Vacation
- Major Purchases (refrigerator, TV, mattress)
- Theatre Tix (I build, spend, then build it back up again)

I'm much more into staycations then vacations, but eventually, I would love to go to New York or New Orleans again, or even Hawaii. There have also been occasions for unexpected travel; sadly, mostly funerals. These are times where I don't want to say no because I can't afford it. I was able to go to my uncle's funeral because I moved funds around. I honestly don't remember from where I moved them, but that just goes to show that when you allow yourself to be flexible with the budget while still living within your means, the sacrifices don't sting as much.

Even if Major Purchases doesn't have the full amount when I need it, I will be that much closer by setting aside a little every month. And on categories like Vacation and Theatre Tix, I will just have to wait until there is enough in there.

While having a budget doesn't necessarily create money, it's surprising how often it seems to do just that.

My financial goal for 2015 was to pay off my credit card debt in full. I did the math and thought, "There's no way." I had about $4,000 to go. But I made it a goal anyway and my Christmas money, my side income money, every extra dollar went to that. One Christmas check included, "buy yourself something nice." The nicest thing I could think of it to do for myself was to get this debt off my back.

I paid off that credit card in full March 1, 2015.

You can also feel more confident in helping your own children navigate finances.

My oldest daughter already has more money in her Emergency Fund than I ever did until about a year ago. She has her own YNAB budget now, and each payday, we sit down together and budget her money. First priority is always putting 20% in her Emergency Savings. Then, we go through what she "needs" before she gets paid again. We set money aside for gas, her auto insurance deductible, car maintenance and car registration, and then give her spending money for entertainment and clothing. She barely looks at her bank account balance, and focuses on the budget categories instead. She has taken from one category to spend from another in between pay periods, and then next pay period, I remind her to fund that category more if she's going to spend more from it anyway.

I've never tried to hide my budget from my kids. When I first tried to show it to them, they had no interest whatsoever. When it was an Excel spreadsheet, every so often one of them would find it open on the computer. They started asking me questions. When I first got YNAB, I showed them the app so that they could see how much was in their category (they would inevitably ask when I was driving). Whenever they ask, I'm open and honest about what a category is and how it gets used. At first, when they asked, they thought I made a lot of money, but when they see everything I have to pay for, they understand when I have to say no sometimes, or not this month.

The common lingo for these types of discussions are, "teachable moments." It's cliché, and it's true. Having that information helped enormously when my daughter got her job and asked for my help budgeting her money. I know it may not protect her against any financial hardship along the way, but it's a good foundation we're building together.

My youngest daughter started asking the places around her school the first week of high school about working there. She was slightly bummed when she found out she had to be 16, but she's still gotten a few odd jobs babysitting. I've let her "blow" that money as she sees fit for the most part because she's already shown patience and determination when she saved her allowance long enough to buy her own laptop. She broke it by not keeping it in the case and throwing her backpack around. I have not replaced it because she didn't need it, only wanted it. If/when she wants another, it will be up to her to fund it.

I started thriving as a single parent emotionally before I did financially. I consider myself thriving financially now because I am out of credit card debt, living on last month's income and have most of my Rainy Day funds right where I want them. This doesn't mean I'm a millionaire, but I can enjoy the occasional night out, can donate funds and goods to causes, and have a positive net worth. Most months, my financial situation gets better. I may not be going to Hawaii anytime soon, but I am content with our lives today.

I hope the same for you.

ABOUT THE AUTHOR

April McCaffery's labels include: single mother of two daughters, paralegal, blogger (http://formerlyaprildawn.blogspot.com).

www.ingramcontent.com/pod-product-compliance
Lightning Source LLC
Chambersburg PA
CBHW070338190526
45169CB00005B/1951